Colourblind! For Kids: Colourblindness Through the Eyes of a Child

Copyright (c) 2015 by Anne Scott Watkinson. All rights reserved.
No part of this publication may be reproduced, stored in a retrieval system or transmitted in any form or by any means, electronic, mechanical, photocopying, recording, or otherwise, without the prior written consent of the copyright owner.

Consultant: Dr. Clara Malinsky, Doctor of Optometry (OD)

Photography: Tim Thomas, Prince George, unless otherwise indicated. Images without attribution are royalty-free images from iStock or Microsoft clipart.

Image on page 15: "Rods and Cones," copyright © 2009. Janet Sinn-Hanlon, Steve Eisenmann; Imaging Technology Group; Beckman Institute for Advanced Science & Technology; University of Illinois at Urbana-Champaign; The Board of Trustees of the University of Illinois. All rights reserved. Used with permission.

Cottonwood Press
2886 Killarney Drive
Prince George, BC
Canada
V2K 3J6

Cataloguing-in-Publication Data:

Watkinson Scott, Anne

                        Colourblind! For Kids : Colourblindness Through the Eyes of a Child/Anne Scott Watkinson

        p. cm.
ISBN-13: 978-0-9939202-0-2
ISBN-10: 0993920209

1. Colourblindness   I. Title

DISCLAIMER

The information presented in this book is not intended as a substitute for consulting a health professional. The ideas, concepts, and opinions expressed in this book are intended to be used for educational purposes only. Although every effort has been made to ensure accuracy, this book is sold with the understanding that author and publisher are not rendering medical advice of any kind, nor is this book intended to replace medical advice, nor to diagnose, prescribe, or treat any disease, condition, illness or injury. Author and publisher claim no responsibility to any person or entity for any liability, loss, or damage caused or alleged to be caused directly or indirectly as a result of the use, application, or interpretation of the material in this book. If you don't agree with this disclaimer, you may return the book to the publisher for a full refund.

For my father, David Scott

and

my mother, Margaret Alexander

ACKNOWLEDGMENTS

Many people were kind enough to allow me to use their artworks, images, or text in this book — thank you so much to Dr. Terrace Waggoner, O.D., of the Eye Clinic at the Naval Aerospace Medical Institute in Pensacola, Florida, and his son T.J. Waggoner (testingcolorvision.com); Marie-Jo Waeber and Gianni A. Sarcone of Archimedes Laboratory (archimedes-lab.org) in Genoa, Italy; Cal Henderson (iamcal.com/toys/colors/); Glenda Price of the Insurance Corporation of British Columbia; Michael Douma (webexhibits.org/); WordRain from www.sxc.hu; Daniel Flück at color-blindness.com; Tony Spalding at colourmed.com; Michael Kalloniatis and Charles Luu of webvision.med.utah.edu/KallColor.html#deficiencies; and Darren Stevenson, Janet Sinn-Hanlon and Steve Eisenmann from the University of Illinois at Urbana-Champaign.

A special thanks also to Dr. Kathy Mullen, Professor, McGill Vision Research, Department of Ophthalmology, McGill University, (Montréal, Canada), who generously shared her time and expertise to provide comments on the book.

My gratitude goes out to Mary Lu Spagrud and her sons Liam and Darian for testing the book — all three made excellent suggestions that significantly improved the book.

To Dr. Clara Malinsky (the "Dr. Clara" of this book), my sincere thanks for allowing yourself and your clinic to be photographed, for providing your expert feedback, and for diagnosing Sam's colourblindness.

I would especially like to thank my family and friends, who provided invaluable encouragement and ideas, and whose eagle eyes caught many mistakes: thank you to Colleen Alexander, Vicky Scott, Eric Scott, George Scott, Tanja Radakovic-Scott, Penelope Scott-McCaig, John McCaig, Stella McCaig, Tess McCaig, Camille Ginnever, Laura Sluggett, Lori Elder, Jean Wang, Debbie Coxson, Carrie Yuen-Lo, Jennifer Bania, Rosemary Dolman, and Peggy O'Brennan. Sam's friend Christopher Coxson also deserves special thanks for being photographed for the book.

To my father, David Scott, very special thanks for believing in me and encouraging me to finish this book (and for your great copy-editing!). The goal of putting a printed copy in your hands helped push me to completion.

To my husband, Andrew Watkinson, thank you for your support for this lengthy project, for your patience with all the weekends and evenings I devoted to it, for being my own private tech support wizard, and for all the backrubs!

And finally, to Sam, for good-humouredly allowing yourself to be the subject of a book, for providing many helpful suggestions, and for demonstrating every day that colourblindness is no impediment to a fulfilling life rich in personal and professional growth — a sincere thank you and a big hug!

IMPORTANT

Don't use the pictures in this book to decide if you're colourblind. Lots of things might affect how the colours in this book look to you, like the lighting in the room (if you're reading this as a printed book), or the way your screen is set up (if you're reading an electronic version).

If you think there's a chance you might be colourblind, please go and see your eye doctor for complete colour vision testing under controlled conditions.

I just found out I'm colourblind. Was it ever a surprise!

My name is Sam and I'm ten years old. I live in northern British Columbia, Canada.

The way I found out was kind of weird.

Our kitchen stove has a clock with green numbers.

One day, I noticed that unless I stood right next to it, I couldn't read the time.

This was a drag, because I like to race that clock to finish my homework faster.

When I told my Mom, she said she'd ask the eye doctor to check my eyes. She said I might be **nearsighted** like her, and maybe I'd have to get glasses.

> If someone is **nearsighted**, they're good at seeing close up, but they have a hard time seeing far away.
>
> With **farsighted** people, it's the opposite -- they can see far away, but not so well close up.

I was excited — I like glasses! My friend Christopher wears them, and I think they look really cool.

Also, I thought they might make me look older, which would be good because I'm short for my age.

But Mom said glasses are no fun. Hers sometimes hurt her nose, and they fog up when she opens the dishwasher.

But I still wanted them.

Christopher's glasses look so cool. I want some too!

A few days later, Mom and I went to see the person who would test my eyes – the **optometrist**.

On the way, I started to wonder what the eye test would be like. Mom told me the optometrist would ask me to read letters on a chart, and would look into my eyes with a bright light. She said it wouldn't hurt at all.

When we got there, everybody was really friendly.

The optometrist turned out to be a nice lady with long red hair. Her name was Dr. Malinksy. She said I could call her Dr. Clara.

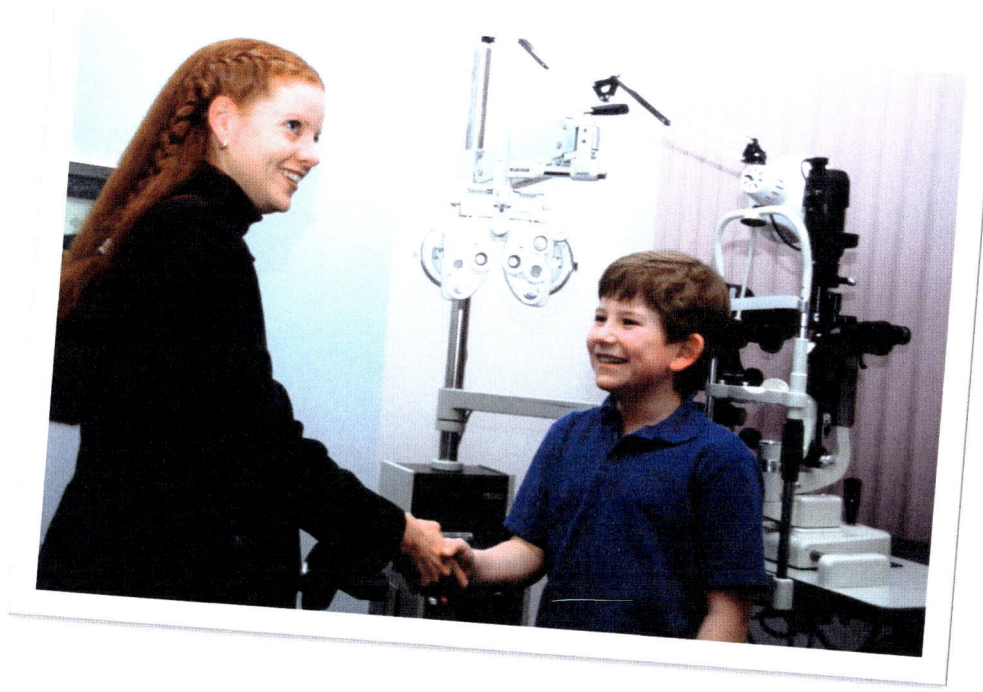

Optometrists test your eyes to see if they're healthy, and if there's something wrong, they can often fix it. They can also help you get glasses or contact lenses. Optometrists have a Doctor of Optometry degree.

Ophthalmologists do everything optometrists do, but they're also medical doctors who know about looking after eyes. They have a Doctor of Medicine degree (MD). Ophthalmologists can find and treat all types of eye problems – they can even do eye operations. When this book talks about **eye doctors**, it means optometrists or ophthalmologists.

Then, the eye-testing started. First, Dr. Clara got me to look at some coloured pictures in a book and tell her what I saw.

They weren't pictures of things, like people or airplanes; they were just lots of little blobs, and mixed in with the blobs you could sometimes see numbers. Later, I found out that these pictures test how you see colours.

Some of the pictures just looked like a bunch of blobs to me – I couldn't see any numbers.

If this happens to you, you should ask your parents to take you to the eye doctor so they can test your eyes.

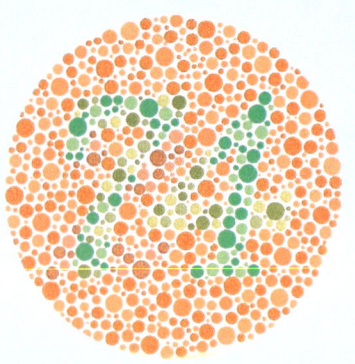

This is one of the pictures eye doctors use to find out how people see colours.

They're called *Ishihara test plates* after the scientist who invented them, Dr. Shinobu Ishihara.

People with normal colour vision can see the number 74 in this picture.

Colourblind people might see the number 21, or no numbers at all.

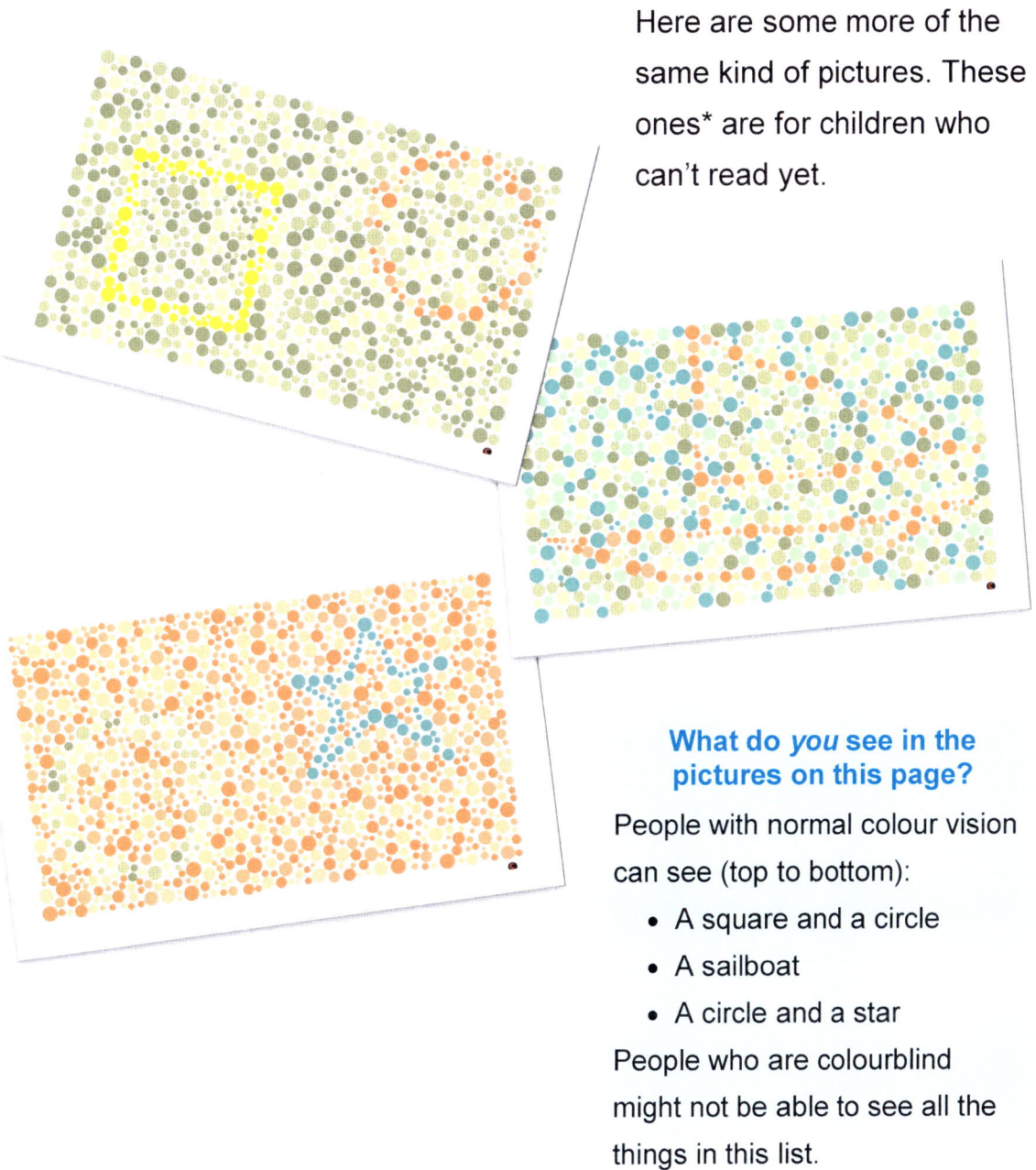

Here are some more of the same kind of pictures. These ones* are for children who can't read yet.

What do *you* see in the pictures on this page?

People with normal colour vision can see (top to bottom):
- A square and a circle
- A sailboat
- A circle and a star

People who are colourblind might not be able to see all the things in this list.

*Colorvisiontesting.com/color5.htm, "New Pediatric Color Vision Test For Three to Six Year Old Pre-School Children," ©2003 Terrace Waggoner, O.D. Reprinted with permission.

Then Dr. Clara took out a long thin box full of little coloured circles.

She asked me to line them up so all the reds were at one end of the box, and all the purples were at the other end.*

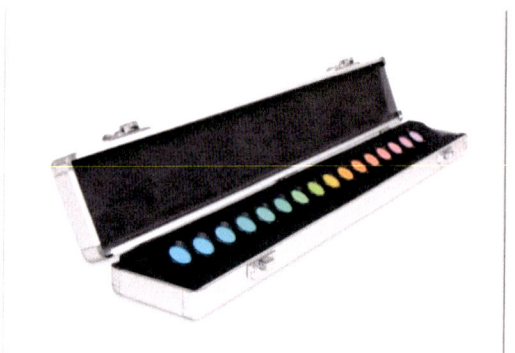

It was hard, because some of them looked like the same colour to me.

Also, I had to do it one eye at a time – she covered my other eye with a patch – so that made it even harder.

But on the plus side, I looked like a pirate! Arrr!

* This is called the *Farnsworth-Munsell Dichotomous D-15 Test*. It helps eye doctors find out if a person is colourblind, and what kind of colour-blindness they have.

Next, Dr. Clara took me into another room and got me to read those eye charts Mom had told me about. I had to read them one eye at a time, and also by looking through a big machine.

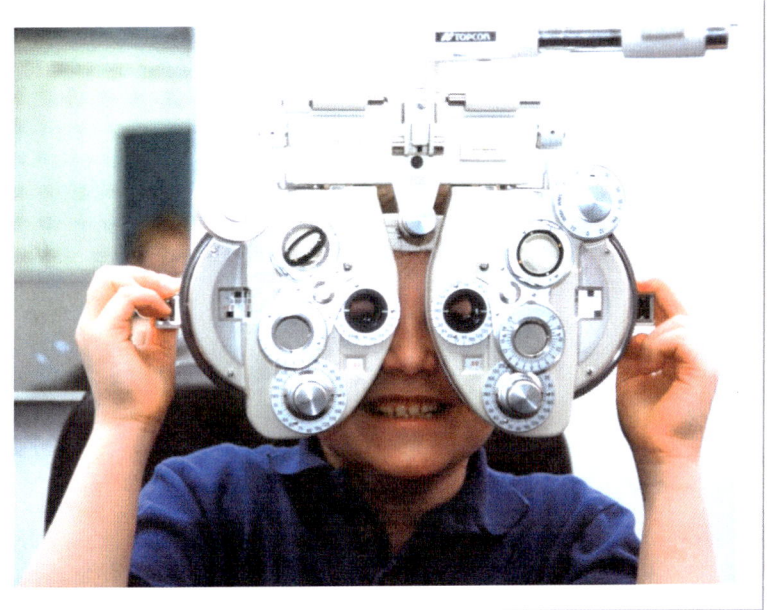

*This machine looks a bit scary, but it gently rested up against my face like a giant pair of glasses.
It didn't hurt at all.*

Eye doctors use charts like this to test how well you can see.

Don't use this one to test yourself, though — the chart has to be a certain distance away from you, and the eye doctor has to be there to do the test.

After we were finished with the eye charts, Dr. Clara put some drops in my eyes to make my **pupils** open wide, so she could look right inside them. This didn't hurt either—the drops just tingled for a few seconds. And having giant pupils was pretty cool!

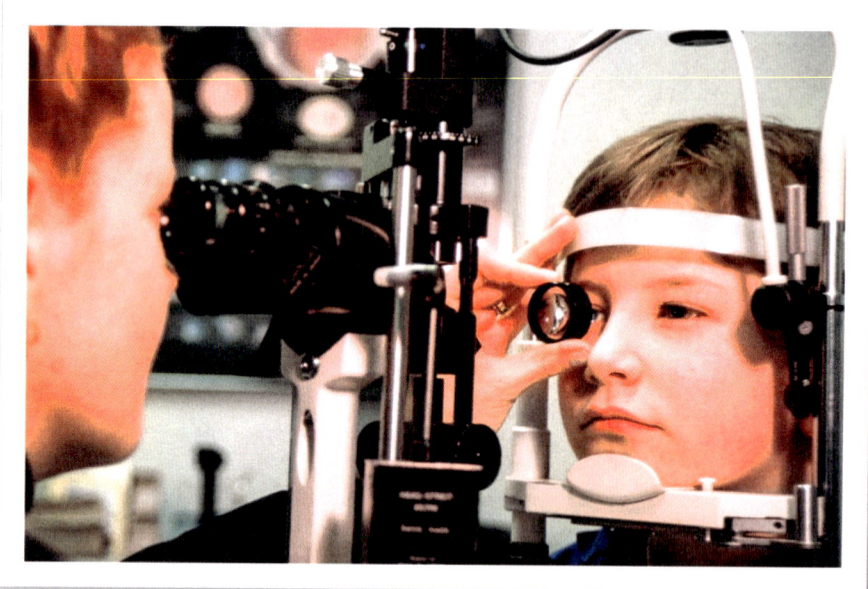

Pupils are the black dots in the middle of your eyes. They're tiny holes, like little windows, that let light into your eyes.

In bright light, like sunlight, your pupils get very small so not too much light gets in. When it's darker, they open wide.

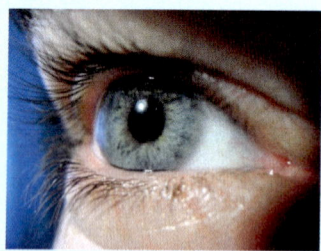

PHOTO: WORDRAIN, SXC.HU

The special eye drops that eye doctors give you make your pupils stay open wide for a few hours. This way, the eye doctor can look inside your eyes with a bright light to make sure they're healthy.

The big surprise was that the eye charts were really easy.

I could even read the bottom line of tiny letters, and Dr. Clara said I had better than **20/20 vision**.

I guess I'm like my Dad—we're both good at seeing far away.

PHOTO: ANNE SCOTT WATKINSON
Me and my Dad.

20/20 vision is normal vision. "20/20" means you can see what a person with normal vision sees when they stand 20 feet away from an eye chart.

Someone with **20/15 vision** has extra sharp eyes. From 20 feet away, they can see little details that most people couldn't see until they got closer (15 feet away from the chart).

And if you have **20/40 vision**, you might need glasses. Imagine a sign that a person with normal vision could read from 40 feet away. Someone with 20/40 vision would need to be much closer—20 feet away—to read the same sign.

But then I got confused: did this mean I couldn't get glasses? And if my eyes are so good, why couldn't I read the clock on our stove? I could see that Mom was wondering the same thing.

Then Dr. Clara talked to me and Mom. She said I was colourblind.

At first, I felt scared. I'm not blind!

But Dr. Clara explained that if you're colourblind, you're not really blind – some colours just look different to you. That made me feel better.

Dr. Clara also said that although most people say *colourblindness,* doctors and scientists say *colour vision deficiency*. Dr. Clara said some people with colour vision deficiency have a little trouble seeing some colours, and some people have a lot.

She said the tests with the pictures and the coloured cylinders showed that I have trouble seeing shades of red. (Eye doctors call my kind of colourblindness *protanomaly*).

She said I can't read the clock on our stove at home because the numbers are dark green on a black background, and dark colours can be hard for people with my type of colourblindness to see.

That's true – I've noticed they sort of melt together sometimes.

Dr. Clara said my colourblindness is very mild, so I'll still be able to drive a car when I grow up. In fact, it shouldn't make much difference in my daily life at all. After all, I've lived ten years without even noticing it.

There are some jobs I probably can't do when I grow up, like being an airplane pilot, because they usually need to have good colour vision.

But I'm going to be a Lego designer anyway, so that didn't bother me.

Dr. Clara also said colourblindness is more common in guys, and if you took a group of 100 men or boys, about eight would have red-green colourblindness (the most common kind).

This is the kind I have – it means you see red and green differently from people with normal vision, or you might have trouble telling the difference between red and green.

(Eight out of 100, wow! There are two hundred people at my school, so I probably know someone who's colourblind.)

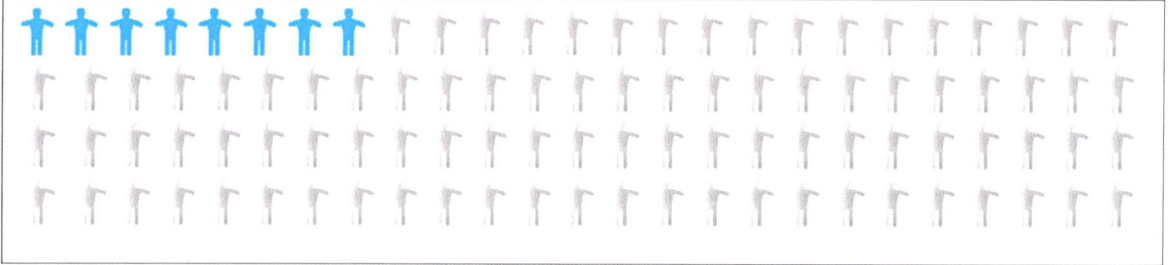

In a group of 100 males, about eight will be colourblind.

How colourblindness works

Special cells for seeing colours

Inside your eyes, there are millions of tiny cone-shaped cells that help you see colours. These *cones* work best in bright light.

(Another type of cell, *rod*s, sees shades of grey. Rods work best in dim light.)

There are three kinds of cones: one for seeing red, one for green, and one for blue. Some colour-blind people are missing one or more kinds: for example, someone might have no green cones.

Most colourblind people, though, have all three kinds of cones — one kind just doesn't work very well.

"Rods and Cones," copyright © 2009, University of Illinois at Urbana-Champaign. Used with permission.

In this artist's image, light enters the eye from the pupil above and hits the colour-sensing cone cells.

These people usually have no trouble doing things that need normal colour vision, like driving a car. Some of them might not even realize they're colourblind!

Then Mom asked how I became colourblind, and if there's any way to fix it.

Dr. Clara said that usually you're either born with colourblindness or you're not*, and there's no way to fix it. But it doesn't get worse either, which was a relief.

She said people inherit it from their mothers. So Mom passed it on to me, even though she's not colourblind herself. Weird!

Dr. Clara said that I probably have an uncle or a grandfather on Mom's side who has trouble seeing shades of red, just like me.

When we got home, we checked with Gumpy and Uncle Lex, but they both said their colour vision was fine. So Mom thinks I might have inherited it from her grandmother's dad.

Mom and I also looked up colourblindness on the internet. We found out that lots of famous people have it.

We also discovered that colourblind people can actually be better at some things than people with normal vision!

---

*Most kinds of colourblindness are the kind you're born with. However, people can also sometimes become colourblind if their eyes or their brains are damaged in certain ways by injury or disease.

Colourblind and famous

- **Mark Zuckerberg**, cofounder of Facebook. This is why Facebook has a lot of blue — most colourblind people can see this colour easily.
- **Bill Clinton**, former US president.
- **Errol Boyd** (born 1891), the first Canadian to fly across the Atlantic non-stop.*
- **Eddie Redmayne**, actor/model/singer (*Les Misérables*).
- **Christopher Nolan**, writer/director (*Batman Begins*, *The Dark Knight*, *Inception, Interstellar*).
- **Fred Rogers**, children's entertainer ("Mr. Rogers").
- Singer **Michael Lee Aday** ("Meat Loaf").
- **Howie Mandel**, actor, comedian, and TV host.
- **Matt Lauer**, host of *The Today Show*.

*Flying regulations weren't very strict in 1930, when Boyd made his flight. Today, it's harder for colourblind people to become pilots.

Cool to be colourblind!

In some ways, being colourblind is like a superpower— there are things that some colourblind people can do better than people with normal colour vision!

Camouflage doesn't fool you

Are you colourblind? In World War 2, you might have worked on a special spy mission!

Camouflage doesn't fool some colourblind people, maybe because they're usually really good at noticing movement, shapes and patterns. When the army realized this, they asked colourblind people to help them find enemy bases by looking at spy photos taken from airplanes.

PHOTO: RAGHU CHUNDAWAT (LICENSED BY ANIMALSANIMALS.COM)

Camouflage challenge! What's hidden in this picture? Finding the answer might be easier for colourblind people. (The answer's on page 26).

"When they found out my uncle was colourblind, they switched him into reconnaissance, and he was used for spotting enemy camouflage in World War II in Europe."

— *Mary Lu Spagrud, BC, Canada*

PHOTO: KIWISINARMOUR.HOBBYVISTA.COM/M4A2.HTM

*A Sherman tank under a camouflage net.
(Italy, World War 2)*

"In a plane at Fort Sill, Okla., an Air Corps observer was able to spot only ten of 40 camouflaged artillery fieldpieces on the ground. An observer of the Field Artillery in a plane spotted all 40 and accurately plotted their positions on his map. The explanation: the artilleryman...was colorblind. Camouflage, designed to deceive the normal eye, fooled him not a whit."

— Time *magazine, August 5, 1940*

You'd probably be a really good hunter

Why hasn't colourblindness died out?

It could be because being able to "see through" camouflage is useful for hunters.

After all, human beings were hunter-gatherers for about two million years.

"I have corresponded with many people who, due to their colourblindness, were the first to bag the deer in a hunting party…

Think of our ancestors, 100,000 years ago… Out of a group of 20…, one man has the fluke of being colourblind, yet his 'disability' allows him to always be one of the first to spot and hunt down the prey.

That means his family is going to eat first…, and his descendants are most likely to survive, preserving the genetic data that passes on colourblindness."

— *Joseph O'Neil, "The Human Side of Colour Blindness"*
start.ca/users/joneil/colour2.htm

You might be able to see better at night

Some colourblind people might have better night vision than normal. For example, one writer describes a colourblind woman who's a ranger at Yosemite National Park in the United States:

"Because of her excellent night vision and ability to spot 'night critters,' she leads nighttime hikes."
— *Coping With Colorblindness*,
by Odeda Rosenthal (1997)

You can see what's hidden in these two pictures (below)

Fool your friends! If you're colourblind, you might be the only one who can see the secret patterns below (The answers are on page 27).

© GIANNI A. SARCONE, ARCHIMEDES' LABORATORY. (ARCHIMEDES-LAB.ORG). USED WITH PERMISSION.

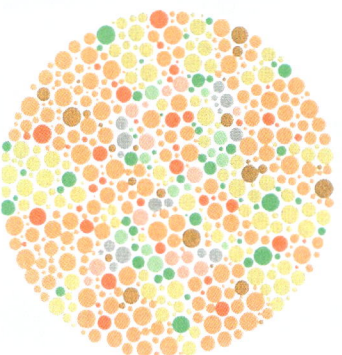

Mom and I also found some websites* that show how things look to people who are colourblind. After we looked at them, Mom said that things do look different to me, but she was relieved to know that I could still see how beautiful the world is.

Normal colour vision

About 92 out of every 100 males have normal colour vision (92%). So do 199 out of every 200 females (99.5%).

Green-weakness (*deuteranomaly*)

In green-weakness, the cones inside the eye whose job it is to see green are there, but they aren't working properly.

This is the most common kind of colourblindness: it affects about 5 out of every 100 males (5%), and 1 out of every 250 females (.4%).

The picture above shows mild green-weakness. Red-weakness, or *protanomaly*, (not shown) is also very common.

*The pictures on these two pages were converted at vischeck.com. If using this website or others like it, note that words ending in "anomaly," like *protanomaly*, mean a milder form of colourblindness (cones that don't work well), whereas words ending in "ope," like *protanope*, mean one type of cones is entirely missing. In other words, know which type of colourblindness you're interested in, and don't let pictures that show a more serious form worry you.

Green-blindness (*deuteranopia*)

In green-blindness, the cones inside the eye that see green are completely missing. It affects about 1 in every 67 males (1.5%) and 1 in every 10,000 females (.01%).

With red-blindness, or *protanopia* (not shown), the colour-sensing cones for red are missing.

Red-blindness affects about 1 out of every 100 males (1%) and 1 in 10,000 females (.01%).

Complete colourblindness (*achromatopsia*)

This type of colourblindness is rare: only about 1 person in 33,000 has it (.003%). These people have no cones at all — they see only black, white, and shades of grey.

It can also make people's eyes very sensitive to light, so that things look too bright and full of glare, as shown above. Because of this, some people with complete colourblindness need to wear sunglasses, even in the daytime.

So I didn't get to have glasses after all, but things are still pretty good. Christopher and I are going to build a giant snow fort today, and if any camouflaged animals wander by to take a look, watch out! I'm definitely going to spot them first!

THE END

Did you know?

Everyone is colourblind in dim light.

Imagine waking up in the middle of the night: You might *remember* what colour your bedroom carpet is, but can you actually *see* it?

At night, it's probably kind of dark in your room, which means you're using your rod cells to see, not your colour-sensing cones. Your rods can see only light and dark, not colours.

So, until the sun comes up or the lights go on, everybody's colourblind!

I can see all the colours that humans can!

I can only see a few. Mew.

Did you know?

Most mammals (like dogs and cats) are partly colourblind (but they can still see blue and yellow).

Most primates, though, (chimps, gorillas, humans, and other related species) have full colour vision.

Solutions to puzzles

PHOTO: RAGHU CHUNDAWAT (LICENSED BY ANIMALSANIMALS.COM)

Page 18: A snow leopard relaxes on a mountainside high in the Himalayas.

© Gianni A. Sarcone, Archimedes' Laboratory.
(ARCHIMEDES-LAB.ORG). USED WITH PERMISSION.

Page 21:

People with red-green colourblindness (the most common kind) will be able to see the word "No" hidden in this image. People who aren't colourblind just see a random pattern.

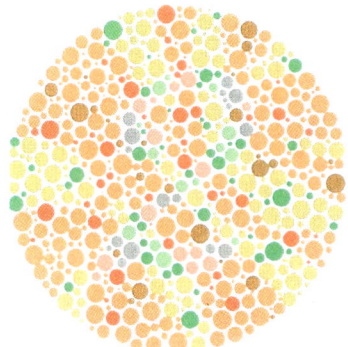

Most people with red-green colourblindness can see the number 2 hidden in this image. People who aren't colourblind see a random pattern.

What's Sam up to now?

Sam is now in his early 20s and living in the city of Montreal in Quebec, Canada.

He didn't end up being a Lego designer after all (although he did take all his Lego to Montreal).

Instead, he's the lead developer at a tech startup company, and also freelances as a web developer, musician, and music producer.

"Life is good!" says Sam.

About the author

PHOTO: ERIC SCOTT
ERICSCOTTPHOTOGRAPHY.COM

Anne Scott Watkinson has been a business/technical writer and editor since 1987. She is the mother of Sam, the colourblind boy described in this book.

She is a member of the Canadian Science Writers' Association.

Made in the USA
Middletown, DE
27 May 2022